FIFTEEN STONES

Other Books by Craig Czury

Non Pensare ai Camion / Never Mind the Trucks, Old School Press, 2016, Soncino, Italy

Thumb Notes Almanac: Hitchhiking the Marcellus Shale, FootHills Publishing, 2016, Bath, NY

Because Although Despite, FootHills Publishing, 2014, Bath, NY

La Cocina de Resolución de Conflictos, ArbolAnimal Ediciones, 2012, Buenos Aires, Argentina

Kitchen of Conflict Resolution, FootHills Publishing, 2009, Bath, NY

American Know-How: Patent Pending, Paper Kite Press, 2006, Wilkes-Barre, PA

Kam Frikê ta Them / I'm Afraid to Say, International Literary Manifestation, 2006, Tetova, Macedonia

Dnevnik Bez Imena / Diary Without Names, Literature Live, 2004, Zagreb, Croatia

God's Shiny Glass Eye, FootHills Publishing, 2004, Bath, NY

In Attesa di Brevetto / American Know-How, Edizioni Empirìa, 2003, Rome, Italy

Technología Norte Americana—Patenente en Trámite Y Otros Poemas / American Know-How—Patent Pending and Other Poems, PapelTinta Ediciones, 2003, Buenos Aires, Argentina

In My Silence to Justify, FootHills Publishing, 2003, Bath, NY

Agliavaizdis / Coalscape, Vario Burnos, 2002, Vilnius, Lithuania

Faces Irreconciláveis / Unreconciled Faces, Red Pagoda Press, 2002, Reading, PA

Closing Out, FootHills Publishing, 2000, Bath, NY

Parallel Noye Technie / Parallel Rivertime, Petropol Press, 1999, St. Petersburg, Russia

Unreconciled Faces, FootHills Publishing, 1999, Bath, NY

Shadow/Orphan Shadow—Sombra/Sombra Huérfana, Pine Press, 1997, Landisburg, PA

Scrapple, Nightshade Press, 1995, Troy, ME

Obit Hotel, Pine Press, 1993, Landisburg, PA

Except..., FootHills Publishing, 1990, Bath, NY

Hacking and Smoking, FootHills Publishing, 1989, Bath, NY

Fifteen Stones

Craig Czury

The New York Quarterly Foundation, Inc.
New York, New York

NYQ Books™ is an imprint of The New York Quarterly Foundation, Inc.

The New York Quarterly Foundation, Inc.
P. O. Box 2015
Old Chelsea Station
New York, NY 10113

www.nyq.org

First Edition

Set in New Baskerville

Layout by Raymond P. Hammond

Cover Art and Design by Kimberly Crafton

Cover Photos by Craig Czury and Kimberly Crafton

Author Photo by John Pankratz

Library of Congress Control Number: 2017937389

ISBN: 978-1-63045-047-2

Fifteen Stones

Acknowledgments

I would like to thank PEN International Chile, Universidad Arturo Prat, Colegio Humberstone, Albright College, Wilkes University, Poets & Writers, Associazione Pro Loco di Soncino, Circolo Culturale Argo di Soncino, and Biblioteca Comunale Aldo Moro di Soncino for their support.

I would also like to thank the editors the following publications: *Poets Speak (while they can) Anthology Series:* vol. 3: *Water,* vol. 4: *Walls; Down The Doghole: 11 Poets on Northeast Pennsylvania; Temple;* and *poetrybay/poembeat.*

For my time in Chile, I wish to thank Hernán Pereira, Pamela Daza, Lucía Ramos, Karen Jogan, Jorge Ragal, Juan Cameron, Eduardo Peralte, Roberto Rivera, and Jorge Manuel Machuca Cid.

Thank you, Ron Friedman, without whom my connection to Soncino, Italy, would never have happened. Deepest gratitude to Aldo Villagrossi, and to the town of Soncino, with special appreciation to Luca Negherbon, Eno Bar, Caffé Teatro, Bar Torre, 3 Ghibellina III, Fatma Demirci, Monica Bray, Riccardo Ulivi, Delia Tinelli, Angelo Bertagni, Mary Brochetti, Elena Vagni, Gigi Roveda, Ariela Pedrini, Paolo Frassini, Alberto & Marisa Ghilardi, Giovanni Bertagni, and to Sami, Katy & Edi.

My thanks also to my writing groups, The Gulag and Old School School, to The Springville Schoolhouse Hooligans, to James and Sue Penedos, Pat and John Atkins, Kerry Shawn Keys, Jenelle Pointer, and to Heather, always.

Introduction

Fifteen Stones is a finely-structured sequence of non-linear thoughts. Time is adrift in the author's fragmented search for "a belonging." Craig Czury is a nomad who crosses physical and metaphysical boundaries, as if he were in permanent spiritual exile: *Was I the same me? People say during the day we don't know who you are...* yet he belongs everywhere: in Valparaiso, Mantova, Soncino, Bethlehem, Vilnius and among the whirling dervishes in Konya; in the voice of Gardel, Caruso or Piaf... *But what language does the subconscious speak?* As was the case for Edmond Jabès, surrealism is Czury's choice to untangle daily tangible nonsense, *drink coffee and write the fog clear.*

If William Stafford's poem *Fifteen,* takes the reader back to adolescence, Czury's *Fifteen Stones* tosses us even further back, into the playground: *looking for a game since a kid. Looking for a moment. A way to fit in.* But perhaps in life, some of us are perpetually out of sync and end up speaking to the neighbor by exchanging lettuce and strawberries.

The literary references and life experiences are brilliantly held together by Czury's piercing sense of humor: *How can I feel less for not quoting Virgil in Latin when Walt Whitman is a service station on the Jersey Turnpike?* He digs the depths with a colorful dagger, reaching the heart without us bleeding. Always seeking truth on singular paths: *If I find you before I go home, I won't go home. I'll already be home. Rumi could have written this, or Conway Twitty.*

Zingonia Zingone

For Kim

Fifteen stones Fifteen flower petals
Neruda's garden in Valparaiso Rumi's tomb in Konya

Fifteen pebbles of sand from the base of Ovid
Fifteen olive pits from Piazza Virgilio

Constanța Mantova Bethlehem Vilnius

Fifteen seashells at the gravesite of H.D.
Fifteen chestnuts Fifteen lumps of blue coal

Soncino clock tower fifteen minutes out of sync
Fifteen minute reprieve when all church bells break loose

For the ones who are perpetually out of sync
Who didn't quite make it Who didn't quite make it back

News from Soncino

I like walking past where people live, hearing music through their windows from another era—Carlos Gardel, Enrique Caruso, Edith Piaf, Robert Johnson... It's in my blood, like the ones who show up in my dreams. I have no idea who they are, but I always go with them just to listen to what they have to say, then I carry their words into these writings. I'd give them credit if I knew their names. Which is another reason my landlady intrigues me. She's a hypnotherapist, and I want to be hypnotized so I can move on into one of my other dimensions. Like moving to Italy isn't far enough? She tells me, her husband interprets, language will make this impossible. But what language does the subconscious speak? Just get me under, where all my real characters are, and so what! I'll come back speaking Italian, right? I think life is that simple, like jumping up while the world is spinning and coming down half-way around, walking these dream alleys with the only comprehensible words guiding me in my head.

This is my town. I'm the mayor signing proclamations around a table in the shape of a casket. I'm the town drunk. I'm the police chief wielding the yellow star of David. I'm pest control running around with a butterfly net. I'm off my leash. I'm off my meds and need a light. I'm the fireman whipping out my hose on Via Borgo Sera. I'm the doctor opening my blouse. I'm the town council outlawing different ways of thinking. I'm my old nag. My old crotch. I'm the teacher whacking my knuckles with a Catholic ruler. I'm the school board banning my books. I'm the disgruntled parent. I'm playing hooky. I'm groping avocados with no remorse. I'm playing dead, mouth to mouth. I'm paying my bills writing rubber checks. I'm old enough to vote for all the names in my cemetery. I'm listening for my name to be called. Even God doesn't believe in God.

I'm not sure who's #1 in this town, the Mayor who's locked into serious conversations, up close in low tones, or the kid who just crossed the street in bakery scrubs, whose brioche I luxuriate in and wash down with grappa.

I nod and say something unintelligible.

I live for anomaly. What is edifying and what is edible... no difference. At a distance, all recipes look like a poem. Up close, nurture becomes second nature.

When I was a dishwasher at the Moscow Hotel, I knew no matter how 4-star the food was, they'd never serve it on a dirty plate. Who's numero uno here? But I always went home alone. On my nights off, with my students at the university and my audience at poetry readings, I never went home alone. Was I the same me?

In Forest City, my friend who's the town hair cutter, never left home except for a stint as a Green Beret in Viet Nam. A lot of people are pulling on him to run for mayor. "Why should I and make enemies, when I influence the entire town from my barber chair."

I nod and lift my glass.

The Mayor's brother's a poet.

The kid from the bakery says *focaccia*.

The Sikhs are playing cricket in a park no American kid today could coordinate and I'm their wayback, the old guy sitting on the cement wall behind the catcher, shooshing the missed ball back to the standby with my stick, or hobbling over to toss it back to him. *Grazia* or *Grazie* or... I'm in the game at a distance feeling like Antonio Machado in that one photo perched on the head of his cane, or maybe that displaced guy in Pavese's poem who'll later gimp off into the night with the forlorn translated what's-her-name smoking. They know I'm not Italian the way I'm eager and watching. I've been biking around my old neighborhood with my mitt strapped to the handlebars looking for a game since a kid. Looking for a moment. A way to fit in. Looking for a way to catch the ball and toss it back that gets me that look. That nod. That foreign feeling I can take home and keep to myself.

Tuesday Market Day in Soncino since the twelfth century. The mayor shakes my hand, says *Bocce.* Vendors under tents are selling clothes I'll never wear. The accordion player is playing *Now Or Never.* O solo mio, the vendors under tents are selling bras and underclothes for women one-third my size. Buttons and sewing lace. Skeins of yarn like a macaroni they call yarn in Mompeo. T-shirts with stupid American logos. Bedazzled sweaters, frying pans, and umbrellas. And umbrellas. The Nigerians are begging for food. I give them money for drink. Salami, salami, salami, fat-marbled, rotund. Bedspreads I'll never sleep under. Pillow covers I caress for someone else's dreams. Apples the size of bocce. The skinned rabbit is fucking the other skinned rabbit. Juiciest dream of nipples... Trout are leaping upstream out of their bed of ice. These strawberries. The prunes are scowling at the dates. Octopus perched like Jacques Cousteau. The figs are nonplussed. Cold damp Tuesday. The oldest cows are growing mold. Gorgonzola.

The Hungarians believe whatever you dress up as for Halloween, a spirit of that costume stays with you for the following year. Your ghost sheets may get you ignored, or passed over for a position. Maybe you become invisible to a lot of people around you, not seen nor heard as clearly as, say, the clown outfit, which has its own serious virtues and backlashes. I'm tooling around these labyrinthian streets on my bike like Evel Knievel when I side-swipe a funeral procession led by the chief of police, who is dressed up as a chief of police. The priest in purple is dressed as the blood of Christ. Two priests in white dressed like wafers. The casket on wheels is dressed for the cemetery with the man inside dressed for the rest of his life. His family, friends, and mourners solemnly walking behind dressed in their long life sadnesses. I salute and peel out over the canal toward home, where I bang this out on my borrowed Underwood, the old way, standing at the up-ended footlocker, jabbing my fingers into uneven stubs, the anachronism I'm already becoming. Scroll, stab, slam, stab, slam, stab, slam, rip, crumple, heave.

The assignment is to draw a picture of your family. Here's my house. Here's my mom. Here's my dad. Here's my... The art teacher tells me to try to flesh out my stick figures, and hands me a stub of chalk. This is really a good idea. I trace the outline of my stick house... it becomes a huge wall. My teacher says good, now position everyone inside this open space to fill the borders. I stand my sister up against the wall and chalk her outline. Really good, Craig, now pose her, and the others, into what they do best, then chalk them in. Here's the chalk outline of my sister tangled around some strange boy in the back of his car... looks like she's at Knoebels on the roller coaster. Here's the outline of my mom spazzing out on the floor with a seizure... looks like she's at the stove stirring a brothy cacciatore. Here's my chalkline dad chasing me through the house with a leather strap... looks like he's fly fishing. The chalk outline of me sneaking out of my bedroom window at night is me climbing the wall.

Imagine there are people who, when they are reading, that's all they're doing, just reading. I have friends who sit transfixed, as if transformed or transported to who knows where, comatose in front of their book. I tell my students, if you're going to be a writer, walk around with a hammer in your hand, wear a tool belt, carry a shovel or a flyswatter. To others, when they see us doing our most serious work, we look as if we're doing absolutely nothing. The punishment is severe. They will hand us a trowel, or a scrub brush or a vacuum cleaner. At least, now that my pen's active across the page, no one will bother me. I understand all of this, between the daydreamer and the poet. For me, once I wade into any strand of words, something inside me immediately starts speaking back. That's when somebody else's words spark my words. Somebody else's story, sentence at a time, becomes huge openings for all of my stories. Memory has no chronology. Your line sparks my opening line, and, after all gets said and written, your book turns into my book. Imagine, there are people who actually wait for another to stop talking before they speak.

Distance always helps reason, sleep on it. Religious, political, economic reasons my grandparents got on the boat to come to America could just be the same reasons to get back on that boat and go back. The courage or desperation in one lifetime to leave everything for an imagined better something something. I used to think it might take maybe five years to learn the language, its nuances and undertones, to figure out everywhere else is just as fucked up or even worse. Oui-ja board Sacco and Vanzetti on this. I think I'd get it now even sooner since everyone screwed down to the floorboards here speaks grappa in loud overtones and gestures. More of a mess than you can imagine. Twenty-five years ago, from Mexico, I saw America as the light from a star long since burnt out. But please, let me get back to you on this after the olive oil and slivers of garlic. After I scale and gut the sardines.

Overcome by the scent of first life, at the fish market I stand glazed in a trance in front of the freshly gutted salmon, trout, squid glistening and sleek. An ancient Piscean hunger to swim back into the womb of the sea. But, at the women's clothing vendor, walking past the undressed mannequin, perpetually young with breasts firm and aroused as my boyhood babysitter's, I have a serious existential question: Which of the two are more dead, the iced fish or the plastic mannequin? The fish because they were once alive? Or the grip of my lungs when she smothers me inside her open blouse? *...an immemorial sap flows up through our arms...* Primordial feelings rising in my blood, as Rilke on the Adriatic puts it... *into the powerful source where his little birth had already been outlived / he waded down into more ancient blood.*

Magpie has become my totem bird, as he sits attentively in the chair next to my table in a restaurant courtyard where I'm having a serious conversation about my future. Yes, the future isn't what it used to be, but he sits nodding and nodding off with his head tucked under his wing. I'm always honored when anyone feels safe enough to fall asleep in my presence, or while I'm reading my poems. One thing I know about the natural world, there will always be a sign when you're most in need. A milkweed tuft drifts past your face. There's a cardinal at the bird feeder. A monarch butterfly alights on your finger to say everything's going to be ok. Like a wink. A secret message only for you. A leaf dancing at the end of a spider's strand between the trees at the edge of the river. That certain glint of light.

It's not impossible, *qui e li e al di la,* to be here and to be there… all the way over there. The lifers know that it's we on the outside who are the ones in prison. For them, the walls have dissolved a long time ago. What I like most about this getting older thing, the inside conversation gets more immediate. The voices… "Oh yes. I know a lot about 'the inner voice'. Once mine starts talking, all the others start up at the same time and they get really loud. They get really loud, then I get tired and I have to go lie down and sleep." We all start laughing. The big guy under how many layers of medication laughs hardest, rattling his chains. The elevator numbers are mismatched to the floor, every floor painted identical. There's a daily security code I never get right. My key, as big as a tack hammer, fits all the locks, I can't always find my floor, my glass room, my doctor. *Excuse me, how do I get out of here?* Poet-in-residence at-large. No, I don't want to know what these guys are in for. Wait, doesn't something inside you freak out when you first hear their crimes? "No, when I hear what crimes they've committed, I start calculating what chemicals are missing in their brains that would cause that behavior, then I start writing prescriptions. I go home to freak out later." St. Elizabeth's fifty years after Pound. I go home to freak out. Writing this from Italy, under how many layers, from my dissonant cage.

Maybe I've gotten too far away from knowing how to fit in, too out of wind, out of the *click* of things. The community orchestra is warming up their instruments. I already know the conductor's going to wreck everything by pulling it all together. I'm here for the sound. All those serious, unknown jazz cats swinging the cacophony of it. I'm the kid in the middle of the brass who can't read music, slicing the air with my peripheral trombone slide vision, developing my what do you call those muscles around the lips for a lifetime of monumental kisses. My impeccable tin ear gleaning notes through the bars.

I sleep maybe four hours a night. Throughout the day I take little naps. I sleep and wake up, drink coffee and write the fog clear. I have another day, several days within one, waking with my foggy thoughts, drink coffee quietly to sort them out. It's the hangover I write myself out of, to fish whatever clarity swarms in the murk. All nerve endings on the surface of suffering humanity. Then I continue whatever nonsense keeps me awake.

I don't know which Italian movie I saw where the professor is venerable and congenial, but I've lingered over the subtitles for decades with the audience screaming, *Don't go in there!*

*

I scream at my college freshmen, *YOU'RE TOO YOUNG TO BE IN SCHOOL!* I give them professorial advice to change their names and run away from home, come back to literature when you're twenty-five, don't get pregnant. I give my serious poetry students professional advice: marry rich. I'm the opening act for the Festival Internazionale di Poesia Virgilio in Mantova. If it wasn't for Mrs. I forget her name, year, and conquest, I would have never heard of Virgil, or Dante, nor have been guided through Hell. How can I feel less for not quoting Virgil in Latin when Walt Whitman is a service station on the Jersey Turnpike? The low half-tones of my harmonica keep me cool with the dead.

Numbers mean nothing to me. *"2+2≠4, only seldom."* Next year I will live one second past my father's death and become a proper noun. In twelve more, I'll outlive my mom and start having kids. 6:15 Sunday church bells, I look at my bare wrist for this kind of clock. The young barista stands in the doorway smoking and texting.

How could any of this have meant anything to us Susquehanna river rats in 9th grade? And why am I here having not forgotten it? As the school children pass by, Who will become the poet? Who will become the auto mechanic? Who will become the teacher just to get even? The demolitions expert? The dog groomer? The cat burglar? Which one will make life so miserable for everyone that there will be long grudges and a lot of blood? I'm a kid out of the late '50s, 1960s Cold War doo wop. When I went to Russia, they too play Blind Man's Bluff, Tag, Hide and Seek, Buck Buck Sasha. Is it the bully who becomes the Prime Minister? Or the bullied who becomes Commandant of the death squad Made In America? Which will become the spin doctor? Which one will be the decipherer of codes? It's a fun game teachers play, cutting out news clippings of their former students, keeping albums, living under assumed names on Facebook.

√*poetry* : *5x5*

5x5 is an online poetry challenge in which a poet is tagged by another poet to write a poem a day for 5 days, each day tagging another poet to do the same. Having refused many tags, I could not resist being flip with one of my best buds, writing multiple poems each day, scratching most, tagging no one.

for J.C. Todd

1

Pythagoras tells us every poem is a theorem: Who I am. Who I used to be. Who I'm supposed to be. Who I think I am. Who I never got caught as. You know, the 5x5 line to line that leads to the Therefore of it all. The Looky Here. Let's get real. You sound like how I feel, we could be friends.

2

A window. A mirror. A pull-down attic door. Bookshelf made out of 14 Stegmaier beer crates. A community bread oven. The poem stops in front of each frame, sniffs, sneezes, then scrolls down. So much better than slapped shut and shelved. So much. Gotta be somebody down there to receive like radio/tv waves in outer space. C'mon! The ink's dried on the tongue, "mummified" as folklorists say, but mystifying scrolled back up embellished.

3

The men I grew up among had no childhood (an American invention since WWII). They had coal mines, weaving mills, factories, wars. I wondered at what age would I become disapproving and dour. I was already agitated and angry. Tones of voices, eyes, gestures. English wasn't my first language, it was the tone underneath the tones of broken English, like poetry, one of the best reasons I always got slapped pointing this out, who I thought I was. There was a better way, but my sister didn't get through that either. C'mon, the big surprise, as I got older I got kinder. I cry at the stupidest human gesture. I fall madly in love with the woman who snorts when she laughs. Only, where I totally don't recognize myself is when I have to flunk one of my students without taking him aside and slapping him awake.

4

At the window of sleep and dreaming, the dead come back looking so much better. I like this mirror. I like this attic door, once pulled down, the dust and grit swallow you. Breathe deep. Mold-caked books. Stink bugs. C'mon, everything you've stashed away in tubs, boxes, or rolled inside rugs has been talking to you while driving in your sleep. How else do you know where to reach for what you left behind with your eyes closed by scent?

5

Today I am walking in increments of 5 like the old days in Missoula, trying to navigate back to the Montagne from Eddy's Club. 5 quick steps and stop, tilt. 5 quick steps and stop, catch my balance on a parking meter. It's a slow zig-zag to the river bridge where it's a swifter careen off the hand rails. I'm doing this with my eyes closed as a tribute to my best teachers, the old railroad bums and indelible souls in Lee Nye's photos hung above the bar and blurred into lifelong conversations. There are still a few of us around in the afternoons during the hours I lecture freshman comp students that they're too young to be in college. Make something happen! Rearrange a few letters of your last names (conflict resolution) and deny you're related. Forever. Split. C'mon, write a 5-page essay (compare & contrast) on a time you lied about where you're going, dressed to fit in with people who scared or excited you and then couldn't find your way home. This essay's due before you're the age of Christ's death. Dismissed.

6

I don't have the heart to pass this 5x5 challenge on to 5 other poets who I know are equally challenged and have better things to do like sit around in their rooms thinking. Besides, 5/5 is my mother's birthday and we're back at it again arguing over the amount of times I ran away from home against the amount of times she threw me out. Even though she's been dead for decades, she always gets the last word in, saying *I had to throw you out because you'd have only run away anyway.* C'mon, if I put 5 poet friends to this task, I'd never hear the end of it, everyone with their beautiful crummy lives. Look at me, Day 3 into this and I can't shut up.

7

This morning, locked inside my 5x5, I'm Harry Houdini,
squirming out of my chains with a massive hangover. All nerve
endings on the surface, probing the right words to figure it
all out once the fog lifts. The key is under my tongue. This is
my best vanishing and recovery act, four days in my bathrobe
with Old Smuggler, waiting for that *click* in my head. I heard
Paul Newman say that once in a movie I starred in, *turns the
hot light off and the cool one on,* and it stuck, like the number
64, averaging the obituaries the other day. Caught me right
down to size old enough and I didn't leave the schoolhouse
all week. C'mon. In Lithuania, there's a delicious potato
sausage, véderai, translates to "shit out, potato in." A most
wonderful mantra to repeat over and over under your tongue
when you're feeling pressed for a prayer.

8

I'm burning a 5'5" painting of the school fire I wrote about when I was running around with the incendiary blond whats-her-name those years when I was hot stuff and the moon over the Pledge of Allegiance at midnight was gasoline. I painted the chalkdust flames on slate the color of weathered tattoo ink. And wrote the fire of your hair across the moon from a schoolhouse where I teach acrobatics on the jungle gym. Where I teach the aerodynamics of striking a match. Where I... C'mon, even if the internet hadn't confiscated this note and read it aloud, I'd still have some kind of future, right?

9

There's a hole in the chain link wire mesh 5x5 you could drive
a Mini Cooper through. Instead, a man decides to climb the
girders and jump into the river. Whoa! That's determination.
What drama! Top this when you're called to punctuate your
white space. When it's time to take the deep swim. What a
legacy he left us, his kids, his followers who are now suiting
up for parkour and deep yoga breathing, looking at the 5x5
cliché of moving from one side of light into another. C'mon.
Like Moses said in both the Quran and the Bible, *Wise up,
there's another path through the reeds.*

10

I live inside the 5x5 flux, in the not-so mean time, as Auden
explains, between being full of yourself saying goodbye and
hello, arriving with all of your expectations, your truest self
lies. Same as catching a glimpse in a store window and not
seeing it's you. I like this most, keeping my passport up to
date. One never knows when an email will invite or a text
will entice. Believe me, I have lost more than one lifetime by
just taking off. There are spice markets in the world that will
make you die for who you left behind.

11

Between the river and the cemetery I have a secret walk
through the alleys no one knows. And if you saw me? I think
I'm invisible, past the sleeping dog and dead squirrel. I take
the trash route. I take the broken glass route. I take the rocks
and rusted metal route, leaning against your beat-up car to
empty my shoe. A phone rings inside a house. Hey, I'm a
burn barrel back alley kinda guy, deflated and who knows
where. I go looking for myself in your tires and overturned
shopping carts. I am a runaway shopping cart with one good
wheel rickety and wobbling toward home.

12

They're just words, they don't mean anything, my beautiful brilliant boy comes home from school to announce, *The moon is a dead rock in space.* He's speaking to poets at the dinner table. The swastika is a Sanskrit peace symbol, bitch. Right? The old guy across the street comes over, *What's the matter with the kid? He was swearing up a storm mowing the grass.* C'mon, Norm, he had his ear buds in, he was just singing.

13

5x5 is a sandbox the Tuaregs built with a fire at the center turning the desert to glass. 5x5 elongated bucket of the Big Dipper. Sieve of light. Sieve of echos. How rheumatic, the poet with the 5x5 hole in his heart sniggers. 5x5 is never 25, only very seldom. In our cube of retention, given to daydream or fantasy, our teachers were the 5x5 block-head refugees of nuns, the G.I. Bill, and state-owned institutions. As Plato clearly points out, *the shadows are dancing, grab the wall!*

14

I'm teetering on the fine lines of a 5x5 between what I know and what I don't know. Between what is real and what my city kids say fake, *that's fake meester* when I introduce imagination. I could fall or fly right now. It's why highwire acts depend on so many *Likes,* checking every second to see if the wire's humming or buckling when the narrow step slips. C'mon, I'm out here on a limb with a cellphone, credit card, and up-to-date passport. You expect me to speak what language?

15

I am at the border crossing waiting for the guard. I have my passport and my privilege stamped 1951. I'm at the border crossing waiting for the guard. I have my good looks and correct English. Charming. I'm at the border. At the crossing. I have my hands at my sides and my shoulders straight. I'm at the border crossing waiting with my white teeth and full head of hair. At the border, I'm at the crossing. 5:05. The watch.

16

From the other side, someone flies a kite over the wall, snips the string. Here's word from home. Someone on the other side. She flies you a kite with love and news she's pregnant. They fly you a kite cryptic with word of the revolution. Someone flies you a kite, drops a pistol. A house key. Wristwatch. A pair of glasses. Here's what's real, 5x5 is all altitude and timing. The stretch.

17

You know, bud, if you keep up the way you're going, you're gonna end up like that character over there, pointing to one of the strung-out hungover guys on the street corner after our haircuts on our way to the Luzerne Legion, where he'd prop me up on a barstool in front of the pinball machine and feed me nickels all afternoon, racking up scores that kept my old man and his buds rolling in shots-n-beers, *This is my son The Character,* until a lot of years later, bucking hay bales up on the Montana Hi-Line, carrying hod for bricklayers in the Nebraska panhandle, cod slinging and pot wrassling on the Oregon coast, pearl diving at the Moscow Hotel in Idaho, fun ride carny, minimum wage among guys who, with dignity, taught me that to *have* character is a high virtue. Your son with character. C'mon! What's it take to change your name and run away from home? I know I keep harping on this, but, strung-out and hungover, what's it take to have?

18

At the stop sign, I don't have a clear view. Baby, how is it your way? *There's a car coming, hit it!* Hmm. Shooting skeet, pull means fling. Scoring tennis, love is nothing. At the gate, the riders on their horses are off. There's a car coming, hit it! C'mon.

19

At the crossing, the gate's down and the train's moving really slow. All the boxcars are wide open, 5x5. C'mon! Don't you want to? What's so precious about your car?

20

I'm wearing a hat. We're wearing several hats. A sundress. We're wearing khaki shorts. Sandals. Walking into the cemetery in sneakers. Sundress with hiking boots. I have a secret memento in my pocket. We have sacred mementos in our pockets. Pool chalk. Bourbon dust. One of us is swimming the lake wide open in the space beyond water. All of us are swimming a wide open space. Thyme-laced carpet of grass. Ayee, this getting older thing, sobbing while singing.

21

It's the same with painting. It's the same with dance, sculpture, choreography, composition... You enter the blank space of the stage, canvas, paper, mud, and dive in because the visions shove you, the voices clarify. I know. At teacher in-services, they all say *Ritalin,* but c'mon, you think we just make this shit up?

22

You put your head to it as hard as you can. Sometimes a solution. Most times the problem. Ok. My sister the suicide had this figured out by the time I was 6. Kept her mouth shut. Didn't say a word.

23

The young and short of it: I have 5 days to make 5 micro fictions happen with kids my age when I flunked 8th grade. This is Fiction Camp. More real than every day at the Catholic university. Lord Buckley, The Nazz. Yes, the statue actually feels like Jesus. Of course I send my students down to the Psych Lab to ear hustle, eavesdrop, capture the essence of conversations. This is Fiction Camp. We're studying dialogue. How to become thinner than hair. We show up in disguise. Scribble and lie when we get asked, May I help you? Are you lost? What are you doing here? *We've been sent here to study the cracks in the walls. They need little people to clean out the air vents.* C'mon, we're kids at the university. This is Fiction Camp. Even you reading this aren't who you're supposed to be.

24

The house next to the fire station is a ground-up tamped-down asphalt 5-something x 5-something vacant lot. I left town on a Wednesday, came back on a Monday and *poof!* The kids who sat on the porch with their toy guns, *Are you a zombie?* when I walked by on my way to the post office, enlisted me as their scout. Of course the town is full of zombies. The woman at the post office is a zombie. The women across the street with 47 cats are zombies. The guys who run the gas station convenient store. I take it back about the women across the street, their cats are zombies. All the gas trucks are driven by zombies. There was a lot of toy gun shooting from that porch. All that Homeland Security. *Poof!*

25

I found the woman who gave birth to me when I was 39. Me, the dangling modifier. She swore me to secrecy to never say *Jake Miller* to her sisters. Ok. Maybe their kids are on Facebook, but c'mon, after she died, at the lunch table with her four sisters, I took off my glasses... undeniably theirs. It was as if a match was struck, immediately recognizing the spit-n-image of their father, a sheet of ice spread across the table. Nobody's spoken to me since. Hmm, great and ancient quandary of the 5x5 mausoleum; in which case, Aldo, Fatma, Luca, Gigi, Kim, I pass this on to the 5xYous. I'm out.

Chilenotes

There are colors that will change your life forever. There's a blue in the Caribbean that will make you come home and rename your children. There's a yellow and a red in Mexico that will make you quit your job and become a jungle painter. I saw a dahlia that made me travel the world in pursuit of Далија and 娇琴纱. The parrots in the mountain trees in Colombia made me wonder if our robins, our sparrows or crows are caged parlor birds in the tropics.

I have a cousin who's a nuclear physicist. God knows what language he speaks. But when he's not splitting atoms, he scuba dives. Astonishing! Imagine what marvelous words he speaks underwater. I asked him one time in an instant message—having not spoken to him for 40 years nor since— and he didn't get what I was after, not at first. Then, after an imprecise number of short clacks about the varying textures of water, light, and the languages of fish, he told me about the controlled precision of breathing and how sound carries throughout buoyancy and decompression, thermodynamics, relativity, and duality with all clarity of coral.

La Casa del Escritor in Santiago. These guys are just like me, they lived it, they wrote about it. So why, having survived it all, when they're finally together, would they want to talk about it! What great camaraderie, humor and strength together in their laughing about things I'll never know about, but can read in their spirit. I like these guys. Except, I'm only here once and I really have to interject questions, because when I get home, my friends will sincerely want to know, *What did you do to survive Pinochet?* From researching their poems and from observation, they have clearly survived Neruda, but I have to ask, What did you do to survive those horrible years? The table winced in unison, but a cry came out from the musician. *M E T A P H O R!* The others exhaled. *We wrote in a parallel language. Pinochet made us greater! We wrote in metaphors unlike the previous generation. There were a lot of metaphors in those years* (one of us blinked at that realization), *a lot of poetry, a lot of music.*

Now I have entered the desert, north of Antofagasta. My bus passes a tanker train the same tawny crud as the graffiti-smeared sand. Out-buildings of mines rust the horizon. Out of a curve, I'm back at the sea. How did that happen! A rocky stretch of desert turns clear sand, stony sand, now volcanic. A perforated magma flow jags into the sea. Bruce Willis explodes the overhead TV screens into blocks of fiery cars, shattered office windows... *Pffft*. Nothing compared to what blew this pato quano wateland out of paradise. I've just entered the moon. The volcano's over my shoulder.

Iquique. I am filming what I should be writing—said the poet who is now a filmmaker. I am writing a poem to a woman who has captured my imagination—said the filmmaker who is now a poet. I am filming my imagination—said the daydreamer pretending a camera. The words spoken in a dream confound the poet—are they his words or the words of the one dreamed who spoke them? The filmmaker shoots a live-action selfie with the daydreamer's camera as he walks into the sea backwards.

With Hernán y Huidrobro at Humberstone Mines. *A train standing on that flat land. A little further out the Earth ends. A whistle drills the air. This is no water game. The wind makes the rigging creak. Winter turns the crankshaft. Flew a dead bird. There were so many things I could not find. I kept finding myself. The clock and a handkerchief dried in the sun.*

Estimado el jefe,

I want to be the *jardinero laureado* of Iquique. I want to write my poems in water from a hose until the sand grows a fuzzy green beard. I want to be Christ-like and water the pigeons so they once again fly. And I also want to water your iron fences with their chained and locked gates so they don't get thirsty and take themselves down to the sea to rust. I want to water your cars so the *cuidadores de autos* have something to polish with their greasy rags. And I want to water your streets and sidewalks for your beautiful homeless dogs in their colorful sweaters to swim through to their mangy scraps. I will water your murals until they gargle and spout mermaids. I won't have to piss behind your bushes anymore. I will hold both hoses out in the open salt air and spray into your golden bursts of sunshine to make rainbows with the mystified eyes of women on either end. The rivulet scars down the face of Cerro Esmeralda will be the lines of my poems. The pages of my book break wave after wave along your shore.

Sinceramente,

OK LET'S GO! I have my bus ticket for Viña del Mar and will arrive after 25 hours, where I'm expecting to be met with gunfire and a riot of dancing in the streets after Chile kicks the balls off Brazil. I am told that the man who will meet me, and in whose house I'll be staying, resembles De Niro in *Taxi Driver*, and he will take me to Neruda's houses in Valparaiso and Isla Negra. *Here I came to the very edge where nothing at all needs saying.* If I don't come home, look for me in the mirror with a quick draw and that smirk.

They are also waving to me goodbye. The man and the woman with their young girl at the loading dock as the bus begins to pull out. My father, my mother and my sister once again sending me off. Yes, I know they don't really know where I'm going. I've been that kind of mystery since I was first handed over. And now, long dead in their long faces, I can't explain either when they *So boy, how can you be going anywhere if you don't know where you're going?*

This is the smell of morning off the Chacabuco line in the hills of Viña in winter, a damp earthy green rust from the corrugated rooftops and woodsmoke at the edge of a park with tall small-frond trees. Blossoming yellow flowers. Cactus. Moss on the concrete I slice into my pocket journal with my knife. Blossoming red flowers and a bird flitting among the rhododendron. One might think, reading this, that I'm a nature poet. In these climes, nature is impossible to neglect. Just remember I'm in Chile. Everything I have just described is a human and social condition, with, in the current "Ministry of Women & Gender Equality," her children building forts.

I'm writing this upon leaving Neruda's house, La Sabastiana, in Valparaiso. I left the rock of my anthracite heart on the shelf in your writing room above your typewriter while the guard looked out upon the port, upon the sea, upon another life further away.

And in the *sala de recibo* off the entrance, I left the breath of H.'s *Papeles de resurrección* and our winged poetry pamphlets *shhhh* between your books where you and Matilda greeted guests, serving them espresso, pisco and tea.

Pretending to be reading the pictographs of the Queen of Sheba above your bed, my knees knocked the mattress Modernaire-style and I felt that middle of the night bed-tremor where something unseen has quietly entered but you don't open your eyes.

I have collected all the stones in your gardens and on the pathway and will claim the weight of my bag at the airport as the eyes of all the seabirds in your poems.

I will hand-deliver one to each of you who reads this, but already, if you know what I'm talking about, my hand is in your hand and these stones are perched in the quick of your thumbnails.

Sitting with Gabriela Mistral on a park bench in Valparaiso, wondering how silence speaks between us. You reading from your solitude what I've written from my solitude. Solace and ignore-ance. Wondering how much of ourselves we recognize in each other at a glance and, finding the woman who gave birth to me, what has always been saying us between cheekbones and eyes, chin and cleft, hair, hairline. Obstinacy and every reason I get slapped for her mouth. A perpetual conversation from birth to silence. Memory, a collective silence. Her ear against my lips I'll call paper for the sake of inheritance. Tongue inside its shell speaking to the sea.

Jorge and I have been waiting over an hour and half for the #610 bus to Viña, saying every swear word we know in English, Spanish and whatever other language comes to mind. The sleeping dogs couldn't give a shit. Jorge shouts at the passing wrong bus *FUCK YOU!* I shout at the next *HIJO DE PUTA!* Jorge hollers *CHINGA TU MADRE!* I shout *QUE CHIMBA CABRÓN!* We are gathering a small crowd who, instead of coins, start tossing their own epithets at us! *ESTUPIDO DE MIERDA! CARABATO! CARABATO Y TU MADRE!* When from the back, a spry, white-haired old geezer, *YANKY GO HOME Pero llévame contigo (but take me with you).*

Yes, now I know it's winter here, suddenly dark, a little past six after a huge dinner of pasta y hotdogs with picante. I'm in bed under tectonic layers of blankets fully dressed in my fleece and scarf shivering, happy to give Jorge, who wants to be called Sr. Cuchilla (is he saying Godzilla?), but is really De Niro in *Taxi Driver,* a break from my spañol ridiculoso, writing this through the frost of my breath, fingers cold. Against the wall, the shadow of the pages in my journal look like wing feathers. The silhouette of my pen between my fingers is a grappling hook.

Chorrillos, a hillside village outside Viña, I think. Across from [Jumbo cencosud Easy cencosud]. Jorge brought me here to ride the escalator, to show me the second level parking garage. I think this is what people who don't drink do. Wait, there's another escalator to... another parking garage! I'm pretending to be in awe of everything I don't know he's saying, which is everything. At the open cement ledge, he points out the drainage ditch, the highway and Chorillos, where I think a woman he loved lived but she went away on a bus. Or is it me who is going away on the bus, and in one of those houses is a woman whose name is Chorrillos he will visit after I go. We have been communicating like this for two days. Best I can do is be awed.

Click

A private distinction between looking and seeing. I'm waiting for the train in Vilnius my friend is hoping not the HIV Kaliningrad to St. Petersburg. *Who do you know would just go into Russia like this on their own?* The U.S. is bombing the milošević out of Belgrade, 1998. It's 1961 and I'm 10 years old. To purify, when you might say my mind playing tricks. To erase whatever I think I know about who I am, who I think I am, like those raku potters changing their names to make themselves new. I don't know what the Bay of Pigs means, it sounds funny. But everyone who says it, *Bay of Pigs,* looks nervous. Everyone tells me when I step off the train in St. Petersburg, if I know any other languages speak them. I am totally enamored of Fidel in his uniform. Fidel surrounded by cheering people. Fidel in his beard smoking a cigar. His brother's name Rauuuuuul. My secret name is Rauuuuuul. A way of deflecting the chide of my vision from figment to mystical. Between what I hear and what I'm listening to. *No one our age, Craig.* Or gift of vision from the other side speaking Sanskrit, hoeing yams. Rousing thousands with my poetry from the balcony of the Hotel Theresa. To rise into my higher next self. Del Shannon driving my heart dead-silly when I *whywhywhywhy* high-pitched like a girl.

A man walks into his bathroom to kill himself, swallows a vial of sleeping pills and walks out to find his wife and kids vomiting profusely. Who's story is this? My friend who's a reporter went to the local high school to cover the Suicide Prevention Speaker who jumped off the Golden Gate Bridge, changed his mind but didn't show up. The speaker didn't show up in the high school auditorium and the janitors went looking for him, thinking he got lost. He wasn't there. That's the point. A man goes back into the bathroom, slits his wrists and walks out to find his wife and kids standing there pale with blood gushing out their wrists, goes back into the bathroom and shoots himself. My friend the reporter lives hand to mouth, has a family, and now has no story to collect on. But she does, and it's a big one. Should be front page completely blank, replete with no high school students waiting for the Suicide Speaker to appear. A man walks into the bathroom and shoots himself in the head, walks out and he sees his wife and kids lying on the floor with pools of blood streaming from their... Here's the story my friend covers: Suicide Prevention Speaker Doesn't Appear, point taken. We go back home without a word, disgruntled. How dare he! Without a word, a man walks back into the bathroom... who wrote this story?... hangs himself from the light fixture, walks out and sees his wife and kids hanging by their necks from the light fixtures. My friend loses out on the story. The grown-ups in the audience get the point and drive back to their crummy lives and maybe yes or no check back in. The high school kids knew all along this loser wasn't going to show up after he ¾ the way down changes his mind. C'mon.

The photographer's hunched over his camera screaming, *That's it!* The same moment Big Nana shifts to her champion bowling pose Miklós Radnóti is being exhumed from a mass grave, *blood mixed with mud was drying in my ear,* his last poem I'm reading in the bulb flash, blood-crusted from his overcoat pocket. Underdeveloped glimpse of Anna Akhmatova staring out of *the torpor common to all of us in those days,* faint smile of the woman who gave birth to me, *her lips blue from the cold. That was a time when the dead could smile.* My old man exhales a plume of cigar smoke, *the afternoon is all fallen plaster, black stones, dry thorns. The afternoon has a difficult color made up of old footsteps halted in mid-stride.* Yannis Ritsos coughs up a glob of tubercular phlegm. That's me, second to the left, spiking my flat-top with the palm of my hand, squeezed between Kafka and Calvino, who prop me up between sense and direction. Of course I'm late for school. Everything I need and reach for as I'm racing for the door breaks off in my hands. When I grab the door it doesn't open. It doesn't open, and I wake up running through the neighbors' yards where women are hanging sheets on clotheslines I brush, tangle, and, pumping my arms, lift myself off the ground, up, clear of the clotheslines, clear of the power lines. I'm treading the air above a crowd of tiny people who are chasing me when I wake up standing in the wings of an auditorium being introduced as a very important person I don't recognize and I've grown a beard. Walking out across the stage I'm not wearing any clothes. The house is packed with everyone in a tux or a gown with hairdos, I walk behind the podium feeling protected as I begin to read from a sheet of paper all the words are mixed up and what comes out of my mouth is gibberish when I wake up peeing the bed I'm covered with seeds it's my birthday and I'm 50 years old all my friends are teenagers

Craig Czury has been conducting innovative life-writing and poetry workshops in schools, shelters, prisons, psych wards, community centers, and universities for over 30 years. A native of the Wilkes-Barre area of Pennsylvania, Craig is also an editor, publisher, and tireless arts advocate. He has authored over 20 books of poetry, many of which are translated into other languages, and he has been featured in poetry festivals all over the world. Craig lives, writes, and teaches in northern Italy and in northeastern Pennsylvania. www.craigczury.com

Photo by John Pankratz

CPSIA information can be obtained
at www.ICGtesting.com
Printed in the USA
LVHW091154230720
661281LV00039B/631